NATIVE PEOPLE ▲ NATIVE WAYS ▲ SERIES

VOLUME I

▲▲▲

The Native American Book of

Knowledge

▼▼▼

NATIVE PEOPLE ▲ NATIVE WAYS ▲ SERIES

VOLUME I

▲▲▲

The Native American Book of Knowledge

▼▼▼

TEXT BY

White Deer of Autumn

ILLUSTRATIONS BY

Shonto W. Begay

▲ Beyond Words Publishing, Inc. ▲

Published by
Beyond Words Publishing, Inc.
13950 NW Pumpkin Ridge Road
Hillsboro, Oregon 97123
Phone: 503-647-5109
To order: 1-800-284-9673

Page Layout: The TypeSmith
Cover Design: Soga Design

Printed in Canada
Distributed by Publishers Group West

Library of Congress Cataloging-in-Publication Data
White Deer of Autumn.
    The native American book of knowledge / author, White Deer
of Autumn ; illustrator, Shonto W. Begay.
        p.   cm. — (Native people, native ways series ; v. 1)
    Summary: Explores the origins of the Native Americans and
profiles key figures in the Americas before Columbus, including
Deganawida, Hyonwatha, and others who have had a mystical
and spiritual impact on the People.
    ISBN 0-941831-42-6 (v. 1) : $4.95
    1. Indians of North America—History—Juvenile literature.
2. Indians of North America—Social life and customs—Juvenile
literature   [1. Indians of North America—History.   2. Indians of
North America—Social life and customs.]   I. Begay, Shonto, ill.
II. Title.   III. Series: White Deer of Autumn. Native people,
native ways series ; v. 1.
E77.4.W48   1992 vol. 1
970.004'97   s—dc20
[970.01'1]   92-12270
                                                            CIP
                                                            AC

I dedicate these stories to my relatives
who are now of the Mystery:
my mother-in-law, Elaine Stately
(Woman Who Sweeps Away with the Crane's Wing);
and my uncles, Nippawanock (Dawn Star)
and Metacomet (Shooting Star)

CONTENTS

PART I

We Have Always Been Here
▼▼▼

CHAPTER 1

What Is a Myth?

The First World was Tokpela (Endless Space). But first, they say, there was only the Creator, Taiowa. All else was endless space. There was no beginning, and no end, no time, no shape, no life. Just an immeasurable void that had its beginning and end, time, shape, and life in the mind of Taiowa the Creator.

— from *Book of the Hopi,*
by Frank Waters

▼▼▼

Like all other peoples in the world, Native Americans have their own stories of how the universe began. These stories also tell of how they came to live on their Mother, the Earth.

"We did not come from Adam and Eve," many of the People insist. "And we don't believe our ancestors came from Asia. We have different explanations of our beginnings."

Before learning what Native Americans believe about their origins, we should first look at two words. They are powerful words, because they reveal how people think about each other. These words are *myth* and *account*.

What does *myth* mean? Many people say that a myth is a made-up story. Others say that a myth is something untrue created by primitive, uncivilized people. These stories were told by men and women who did not know the "true" story. Still others say that myths are legends of "dead gods."

What about the word *account*? Most folks have more respect for this word. It implies truth. The Bible's story of how God created the Earth and made Adam and Eve, for example, is widely held to be an "account." People who believe in the truth of the Bible believe that its stories are accounts rather than myths.

The Hopi Indians, who live in the states of New Mexico and Arizona, have an account of the creation of the Earth different from the one in the Bible. Hopi tribal elders explain to their children how Taiowa, the First Cause of All — the Great Mystery — created Sotuknang. Sotuknang created Spider Woman to be his helper. Together they created life out of the First World. In a great sea of sounds, they caused things to stir and move about with a sacred "spirit-knowing" that kept them still close to Taiowa.

Are the Hopi elders telling a myth to their children? Or are they passing down a cherished account?

A person doesn't have to believe an account is true, but he or she should respect another person's belief. Out of respect we should call the Hopi story an account. If we call it a myth, we are implying that it is false or wrong. It may be wrong for us, but for the Hopi, it is true.

All Native American tribes have their own accounts of how the world was created and of how they came to be. Many of these accounts are similar, but in some ways they are different. The Cherokee account differs somewhat from the Sioux. The Sioux account differs from the Apache. And they all differ from the one in the Bible.

Native Americans were taught to respect the religious beliefs of others. Unfortunately, Native American beliefs have not been respected in the past.

The People say, "Missionaries have told us our beliefs are wrong, that we should believe in their beliefs. We don't tell the missionaries that they are wrong. Their faith is right for them; our beliefs are right for us.

"This is how things came to be," the People explained in different ways. "Some of us emerged from the earth on a reed that led through an opening; others came out of a hollow log. Some descended from a woman who fell from the sky and gave birth to twins." But in all accounts, the People have told how we were formed by this ancient land. "By the sweeping winds. By the mighty sun. By the great waters. Even the stars we stand in wonder beneath had influence in our origins. That's how we came to be what we are, the People."

To the Native American, "We have always been here."

CHAPTER 2

Mother Earth

▲▲▲

I wonder if the ground has anything to say? I wonder if the ground is listening to what is said?. . . The ground says, It is the Great Mystery that placed me here . . . to produce all that grows, the trees and fruits. The same way the ground says, It was from me that man was made. The Great Mystery, in placing men on the earth, desired them to take care of the ground and do each other no harm.

> — from Young Chief, of the now-extinct Cayuse people, who once lived in the area of present-day northeastern Oregon and eastern Idaho

▼▼▼

Native Americans believe that Mother Earth formed us, both physically and spiritually. The earth is our mother. We respect and love her. She provides us with food, clothing, and medicine. We were taught to do nothing to harm her.

We were also instructed to respect our animal, bird, tree, and plant neighbors. To us, they are relatives, for we all share the Great Mystery of life and the same mother.

We call the squirrel "brother," we call the hawk "brother"; we call them "sisters." We call the sun "grandfather" or "older brother." The moon we call "grandmother."

That's why city life can frighten Indians. In the city even Indians with strong traditional ties to Mother Earth can lose contact with the land. In the cities they are surrounded by people, surrounded by buildings — cut off from nature.

Everywhere people speed along highways or walk on concrete sidewalks. They no longer feel the soft earth beneath their feet. On both sides of city streets, canyons of buildings block out the sky. At night, bright city lights make the stars disappear.

For thousands of years the Mayan Indians lived in the jungles of Mexico and Central America. For more than 3,000 years they developed their civilization. Fifteen hundred years ago they began to build large cities in the jungle, cutting huge stones for their buildings by hand.

While Europe was going through its Dark Ages, the Mayan Indians created a Golden Age. It lasted for more

than five centuries. During this time, the Mayas constructed stadiums where ball games were played. They built towering temples to honor and address their gods. They built observatories to study the stars. They were the first to develop a calendar as accurate, and more complex, than the modern one we have today. They had one of the most advanced cultures in the world. Then, mysteriously, they left the great cities and went back to the jungle, where many of their descendants still live.

Some of the old ones, the native elders, say that the Mayan Indians deserted their cities because they feared what those cities were doing to them. Accounts of the Mayas say their priests saw what living in a crowded city can do to people. Somehow they got the People to leave.

Anthropologists (people who study groups of people) and archaeologists (people who dig in the earth looking for artifacts of ancient civilizations) have different theories about why the Mayas disappeared from their cities, but no one can prove them. What the Indians themselves say makes good sense.

Use your minds and hearts and try to understand how the Indian feels about nature and the land.

"Sit down here. All of us, on this open prairie, where we can't see a highway or a fence. Let's have no blankets to sit on, but feel the ground with our bodies, the earth, the yielding shrubs.

"Let's have the grass for a mattress, experiencing its sharpness and its softness. Let us become like the stones, plants, and trees. Let us be animals, think and feel like animals.

"Listen to the air. You can hear it, feel it, smell it."

These are the words of Lame Deer, in the book *Lame Deer, Seeker of Visions*, which he wrote with Richard Erdoes. Lame Deer was a Sioux medicine man who lived on the Pine Ridge Indian Reservation near Rapid City, South Dakota, until his death in 1976.

Today, while we witness the destruction of the land and our environment, more people are realizing how right the Native American is. We need to respect Mother Earth. We need to take care of her. We need to feel a part of her again. No longer is this only "Indian" thinking.

CHAPTER 3

Who Are the Native Americans?

▲▲▲

Whether we are called Native Americans, Indians, Cherokees, or Crees, we know what we are. Our devotion to Mother Earth and our awareness of the relationship we have with the Great Mystery make us what we are. All this, all this calls us back to our ancestors.

— White Deer of Autumn

▼▼▼

In 1519, Hernán Cortés, a Spaniard, invaded Mexico. He and his men brought with them a belief in the biblical account of the creation of the world. Nothing in the Bible, however, had prepared these soldiers for the tribes and nations of Indians they would find. Nor were they prepared for the splendid cities they would discover. The Old Testament, in telling the story of creation, never mentioned the Indians and their achievements.

What Cortés and later explorers found were very advanced cultures. They saw beautifully built temples and colorful pyramids, observatories to study the heavens, huge stone carvings, libraries for books, and finely crafted ornaments of gold and silver.

So, the explorers and their countrymen who followed them created myths to explain the existence of the Native Americans.

In 1641, Antonio Montezinos, a Jewish Portuguese adventurer, visited South America. When he returned to Europe, he wrote a book, *The Hope of Israel*. The lost tribes of Israel had somehow crossed the Atlantic Ocean and settled in the Americas, he told his readers. For 200 years much of Europe accepted this.

Two hundred years later, for many Europeans, the Native American was no longer Jewish. He was Egyptian. Somehow, Egyptian sailors had sailed their small reed boats to the New World. They brought with them the knowledge to build great cities and pyramids. After all, they said, weren't there similarities between the monuments in Egypt and Mexico? And didn't the Aztec Indians look like Eygptians?

Later, some writers suggested that sailors from Phoenicia (in ancient times, this was the name given to the seacoast of Syria and Lebanon) shipwrecked in Central America. Others suggested that Irish monks visited

the New World and gave the natives the necessary knowledge.

A few even suggested that Native Americans came from Atlantis. The continent of Atlantis supposedly existed thousands of years ago but was destroyed. It is said that before its destruction, the survivors escaped to South America.

Another explanation for the Native Americans' existence has to do with a mythical land called Mu. Some writers have placed this continent in the Pacific, and it too was destroyed. They said Native Americans came from there.

No hard evidence exists to support any of these myths, but the Europeans and their New World descendants kept trying to explain where Native Americans came from and who built the remarkable structures found in the Americas. They do agree on one thing: Certainly the Indians could not have done it by themselves. The Indians were "ignorant savages."

In the early 1960s, several American writers explained the Indian achievements in a new way. They said that visitors from outer space came and taught the Indians how to build fabulous cities and monuments.

Few people seem willing to say that Native Americans were smart enough to have created such advanced civilizations. A well-known scientist once remarked, "These cultures could have never been accomplished by savages."

CHAPTER 4

Digging for Answers

**During the last hundred years, archae-
ologists have been sifting the soil of the
Americas. They have been trying to discover the origin of Native Americans.
Although the research continues, most
have concluded that Native Americans
came from Asia.**

— White Deer of Autumn

▼▼▼

According to archaeologists, ten to forty thousand
years ago small bands of Asians migrated across
the Bering Strait into Alaska. They used a land bridge
that existed at the time. This land bridge was created
when the Earth turned much colder. As the land and
water began to freeze, the level of the sea dropped hun-

dreds of feet and a strip of land was uncovered between Asia (off the coast of Kamchatka and Siberia) and Alaska. Bands of Asians then traveled across North America and into Central and South America.

Forty years ago, school textbooks taught that Native Americans came across the Bering Strait about 5,000 years ago. But as archaeologists uncovered more Indian gravesites and discovered more artifacts, the dates of arrival began to change.

First, the arrival date was pushed back from 5,000 to 10,000 years ago. Then, in the late 1950s, Dr. Juan Armenta, a Mexican paleontologist (a person who studies fossils and ancient forms of life), uncovered stone tools and animal bones in Valsequillo, near Puebla, Mexico. The animal bones had hunting scenes carved on them. Close by, Dr. Jose Luis Lorenzo discovered other signs of humans living in the area. The bones and other artifacts were dated at 27,000 years old.

Archaeologists now generally accept 40,000 years ago as the arrival date of the Indians. But even now the dates are changing. In 1968, Louis S. B. Leakey, a world-famous anthropologist and archaeologist, was digging a site at Bat Cave, New Mexico. Leakey discovered primitive stone tools called "pebble choppers." Pebble choppers are hand-shaped stones used as tools to chip flakes off of flint to make arrowheads and spear points. Leakey dated the pebble choppers to be at least 40,000 and possibly as much as 100,000 years old.

Leakey also located another site at Calico Hills, California, just east of Barstow. Evidence uncovered there supported his belief that Native Americans had been living on the North American continent for at least 200,000 years, possibly 500,000 years!

CHAPTER 5

Is the Migration Theory Backwards?

In the real beginning Wakonda made the People: men, women, and children. After they were made Wakonda said "Go!" So the People took all they had, carried their children, and started toward the setting sun . . . .

— from an Omaha Indian
creation account

▼▼▼

In the winter of 1798, one of the great Miami chiefs, Little Turtle, was in Philadelphia to discuss the Greenville Peace Treaty with Quaker leaders and members of Congress. While he was there, he met a Frenchman known as Count Volney. Count Volney took a special interest in talking with Little Turtle.

One night, Count Volney presented Little Turtle with a map of eastern Asia and America. The Frenchman was amazed at how Little Turtle, whom he called the "savage," immediately recognized Lake Michigan, Lake Superior, and the Wabash and Mississippi rivers. According to Werner Müllers's book, *America: The New World or the Old?*, Count Volney pointed to the Bering Strait and explained to the Miami chief how the original Americans, Little Turtle's ancestors, came from Asia, "crossing a land bridge or moving along the Aleutians from Asia." Count Volney did this to prove his point that the Tartars (people from Persia, some of whom lived in Philadelphia at the time) were similar in physical appearance to Little Turtle's people because Little Turtle's ancestors came over from Asia.

Writes Müller: "Little Turtle quickly grasped what was meant and shrewdly exposed the weak point: 'Isn't it possible that the Tartars, who resemble us so closely, came from America? Is there any evidence to the contrary? Why shouldn't we have been born here?' "

Nearly 200 years later, modern-day scientists cannot answer that question any better than Count Volney could have. In fact, the most recent evidence suggests that what Little Turtle believed is more likely than what Count Volney assumed.

Like Louis Leakey's Calico Hills discovery, these recent finds were located in California, and like Calico Hills, they too have stirred the minds of scholars. Several human skulls unearthed at a San Diego site were dated to be 48,000 years old by two of the most widely used and modern methods known to science. These are radiocarbon testing (measuring traces of radioactive carbon or C-14) and racemization (measuring changes in amino acids). Each method tests for a substance found in something that was once living, such as a piece of wood, a bone, or a human skull. The surprising nature of these 48,000-year-old California skulls is that they are "fully modern." This means they are like ours.

Another skull, found in Sunnyvale, California, just west of San Jose, is so old that it has no radiocarbon left for carbon-14 testing. It is dated to be at least 70,000 years old!

According to archaeologists Jeffrey Goodman and other researchers, these skulls are the earliest evidence of fully modern humans (Homo sapiens) in the world.

Goodman believes that modern man began in North America and that fully modern humans developed separately in the Americas and eventually traveled to Asia.

Although the late Miami chief Little Turtle and the modern archaeologist Jeffrey Goodman share common ideas about the origin of Native Americans, these ideas, including Goodman's evidence, have not been accepted by most archaeologists. They find these ideas too radical.

Yet, there is other support for the theory that Native Americans have been here at least since the origin of fully-modern man. This support comes through the scientific study of blood. According to *The American Heritage Book of Indians*, by William Brandon, "Blood group studies of American Indians have recorded the purest type-A groups in the world, as well as the only known populations entirely lacking A; the purest O groups in the world; and the purest B group in the world. An eminent geographer concludes that the basic peopling of the Americas may have taken place 'before the primordial blood streams of man became mingled.' "

Brandon goes on to write, "One thing is obvious: if the American Indians can claim descent from those early people of 15,000 – 20,000 years ago, and some undoubtedly can, then they are by far the oldest known race on earth. There is no evidence of the identifiable appearance of any of the other modern races, Mongolian, white, or Negro, until much later."

Perhaps 100 years from now, the knowledge of scientists and scholars studying the origins of Native Americans and of humans in general may be totally different.

But one thing is certain: Until the actual evidence is proven in hard scientific fact, the Bering Strait migration as an explanation to the origin of Native Americans is, at best, a theory. It is not fact.

Until then, Native Americans are perfectly content to believe what the People have always said: "We have always been here. We were created from the earth and her waters, and we progressed as a people on this land."

CHAPTER 6

Robbery

▲▲▲

I have killed the deer; I have crushed the grasshopper. I have cut the hearts out of trees growing old. In my life I needed death to live . . . . When I die, my body returns to the earth to feed the grasses and nourish new life . . . . In this way, the Circle of Life is never broken.

> —from "I Have Killed the Deer," a song of the Taos Pueblo Indians, who live in the present-day state of New Mexico

▼▼▼

Scientists seem obsessed with finding answers to the origin of Native Americans and of humans in general. To find these answers they scour the slopes of canyons. They drill into the earth. They take the bones and sacred objects from the graves of Native Americans.

Once a burial site is "discovered," the race begins. Who can remove the objects first? Sometimes archaeologists find them first. They use them to pursue their search for information. Sometimes grave robbers arrive first. They remove the skulls and other objects in order to sell them.

Where do these skulls, skeletons, and sacred objects go? Sometimes they go to private homes, sometimes to museums. Sometimes they are stored on shelves in laboratories.

Sometimes a state or province builds a museum at the grave so that everybody can see the remains.

To many Native Americans, the removal from the earth of bones and the objects buried with them is grave robbery, whether it's for archaeological research or for resale. It is just as deplorable as the digging up of a grave in the local church cemetery. People should begin to question why the graves and remains of our ancestors are violated. Is this necessary?

In some towns and cities in the Southeast, Indian mound graves have been destroyed when bulldozers dug them up to use the shell-packed soil to build nearby roads.

In St. Petersburg, Florida, one amateur archaeologist removed the skeleton of a young Indian girl from an earthen mound. He discovered that she was buried in the fetal position (the curled position of a baby in the mother's womb). He also removed valuables from her grave. Then he hung the remains in a back room in his office and used them as a joke to frighten people.

The skull of Osceola, a famous Seminole chief from Florida in the the early 1800s, was removed from his grave. A dentist in Charleston, South Carolina, used it as an ashtray.

In August 1989, in Albuquerque, New Mexico, Susan Harjo, the Director of the National Congress of American Indians, urged museums to return thousands of Indian skulls to the tribes. Many of these skulls had been collected by the U.S. Army in the 1800s. The Army wanted to do cranial (head) studies.

The Army collected thousands of skulls of our ancestors. Archaeologists have collected thousands more. Who knows how many thousands have been removed by other people! These skulls are part of the sacred remains of our ancestors.

The People say, "We do not remove the remains of other people. We respect their graves. We ask for the same consideration."

Many Native Americans feel that no one should disturb the graves of the dead — for any reason. They should receive the same protection and respect shown to graves with tombstones on them. The skulls and other bones of departed Indians should not be treated with disrespect. They should not be used as attractions. They should not be hung in offices. They should not be used as ashtrays. They should not collect dust on the shelves of the laboratories of scientists. They should be returned to the earth, our Mother.

"The earth is our Mother," the People insist. "When we die, we give our bodies back to her to return to the soil, to nourish new life. In this way, the Circle of Life is not broken."

CHAPTER 7

The Destruction

▲▲▲

**Weeping, I, the singer, weave my song of
flowers of sadness;
I call to memory the youths . . . gone to
the land of the dead; once noble and
powerful here on earth,
the youths were dried up like feathers,
were split into fragments like an
emerald . . . .**

— from an Aztec poem

In 1519, the soldiers of Cortés imagined they were
dreaming when they came upon the Aztec city of
Tenochtitlán. Nothing they had ever seen in Europe could
compare to the splendor of this place. The Aztec capital
was almost completely a floating city. Everywhere were

little islands of floating gardens. Between these were canals that the Aztecs traveled in dugout canoes.

The city and its neighboring communities had more than 300,000 people and more than 60,000 houses. (It was about five times bigger than London, England, was at that time.) Inside the city were great pyramid temples and a magnificent palace.

Cortés admired the spendor of it all, but he had no doubts about the People. They were "heathen." They did not share his religious beliefs. In order for Cortés to steal their wealth, they had to die. And die they did — by the thousands. Within five years he would lay to ruin Tenochtitlán and crush its people. Later, the same stones of the Aztec monuments would be used to build the great Metropolitan Cathedral of Mexico City.

It's hard for us to realize that so much of the American Indian knowledge and culture was destroyed by the early European explorers and immigrants. Like Cortés, they made few efforts to understand the Native people.

All over the Americas this destruction took place. Temples were plundered. Religious objects cast in gold and silver were melted by the Spanish and other Europeans into gold bricks and sent back to Europe.

One of the most horrifying acts in history occurred when the wonderful libraries of the Mayas and Aztecs were burned. It began in 1562, when a Catholic priest, Diego de Landa, felt he had to destroy the writings of the Devil. He viewed as "devilry" the Native sculptures of snakes and the temples where the "plumed-serpent" was honored. He understood nothing of the cultural hero

Quetzalcoatl, who was called the "feathered" or "plumed serpent" by the People.

Under friar Diego de Landa's orders, the Mayan libraries were gutted. In one "book-burning ceremony," thousands of Mayan books were brought to the town of Mani in the Yucatán. There the books were built into a great pyre and torched. They were burned by the thousands because they were written by people who did not share the same faith as the Spanish.

Friar de Landa also ordered soldiers to hang "many Indians" by their feet and some by their arms. While being tortured by the friars, the Indians were forced to watch the destruction of their cherished books.

Similar fires were fueled by Aztec books as the conquerors' burnings spread into Mexico. The Aztec books were cared for by their priests with the same care in which one tends a garden of flowers, for poems to the People were symbols of flowers. Only fragments of some of them survived the Spanish. Among them was the book of flowers of Huezotzincos. Such a book was considered a "bouquet of words."

Of the thousands of Mayan books that were burned, only parts of three were saved. One has to do with astronomy. It is called the Dresden Codex, because it was discovered after World War II in the state library of Dresden, Germany, by Russian soldiers. They carried it to Moscow for study. The other two surviving books are now known as the Madrid Codex and the Codex Paris. Both volumes are named for the cities where they are kept.

According to scholars, each book appears to be deeply concerned with ceremonies, rituals, and prophecies.

We can't begin to know what was lost in those fires. Much of the Native knowledge of medicine and astronomy, as well as their great poetry, is gone.

"Our priests wept," the People said, their faces wearing masks of pain. "How do we mourn for such a loss? Nothing could have been as cruel as the burning of our books — except the enslavement of our children. And the children, we would hide them or carry them into the forest. Mothers who couldn't escape would smother their infants rather than have them stolen for slavery.

"But the books! We could not stop the fires. We could only cling desperately to our memories and weep. They took generations of our hearts and minds, the books, and they threw them into the fires. And we could not stop them."

And so it was. The wisdom of ages disappeared in the black smoke of burning books.

CHAPTER 8

Gifts of the People

▲▲▲

The Indians usually lived in small bands and wandered about from place to place.... They were mostly quarrelsome. Some of the different tribes or bands had settled homes and were partly civilized, but most of them were wandering savages who did nothing to develop this great country.

— from "Twenty-five Lessons in Citizenship," a pamphlet printed in 1969 in Berkeley, California, for people filing applications to become U.S. citizens

▼▼▼

How did the Native Americans like the Aztecs, the Mayas, and the Incas construct the largest pyramids in the world? How did they know the concept of the zero, centuries before anyone else in the world? How were the Incas able to cut huge stones weighing tons and place them together so that a piece of paper could barely fit between them?

Their books and their civilizations are gone, so we may never know for sure. But some pieces of the past remain. We know that the Aztecs and the Incas, for example, were unsurpassed craftspeople. They adorned themselves with delicately designed ornaments of gold. They believed that gold was the excrement (waste) or the "sweat of the Sun." By wearing gold, they showed their humility before our mighty star. Many Europeans, however, went crazy over gold. To them it was wealth.

How the Indians shaped gold and other metals is largely a mystery. The Spaniards believed that gold was very valuable. But the Incas' workmanship of the precious metal was even better than the gold itself.

The Native Americans of the southern Americas were renowned astronomers as were the Pawnee of the North American Plains. They measured star movements. They predicted solar and lunar eclipses. They marked the exact moments when the seasons changed.

At Chichen Itza, in the center of the Yucatán Peninsula of Mexico, the Mayan Indians built a tall pyramid now called El Castillo (The castle). On each of the four sides it has a staircase leading to the top. To reach the top, a person has to climb more than one hundred steps. Once there, he or she can see all the other buildings in the area.

At the bottom of the building are large snake heads. The snakes' bodies are made from triangular stones that go up each side of the staircase. At the exact moment of the summer solstice (when the sun is at the highest point in the sky), the stones of the snakes' bodies appear to move down the staircase. At no other time do the snake bodies appear to move. That was how much the Mayas knew about astronomy!

Indian knowledge of plants for food and medicine revitalized the world. Machu Picchu, in the Andean Mountains of Peru, was the Incan agricultural center. It was here that many of the foods which feed the world today were developed.

The Native Americans were also master builders. From fine temples to pyramids to entire cities, the Indians built with incredible skill. They adorned these structures with beautiful artwork.

Over a thousand years ago, in New Mexico's Chaco Canyon, Native Americans called the Anasazi built Pueblo Bonito. It was the world's first giant apartment building. Standing five stories tall, it covers more than three acres and contains 800 rooms.

Not until the late 1800s was an apartment building in New York City built larger! Pueblo Bonito wasn't the only one constructed by the Anasazi. There were over a dozen houses like it in the area.

But the grandeur of Pueblo Bonito was not merely its size. It was nearly a perfect environment. Because of its design and location in relation to the sun, it had a comfortable climate. It also marked the beginning of seasons, and it provided kivas (small circular rooms) in which people could meditate or chant their prayers.

Some of the descendants of the Anasazi are now called the Pima. Anthropologists have called their society one of the most peaceful in the world. The Pima developed the famous Pima cotton that is now grown in Egypt.

Another magnificent achievement is the Gila River canals in Arizona. The Hohokam Indians dug these canals to bring water to the desert. With the canals, the Hohokam were able to turn the desert into productive farmland. The engineering of the Gila River canals is one of the Western Hemisphere's "wonders of the world."

In the Ohio Valley, Native Americans built a large number of huge mounds. Their civilization has thus been called a "mound metropolis." The great Cahokia mounds, where the city of St. Louis is today, covered 125 square miles. Upon them were built structures of prayer and ceremony. Surrounding the massive mounds was a metropolis with a population of 40,000.

In the Northeast, the Iroquois people, or Haudenosaunee ("People of the Longhouse") — the Onondaga, Mohawk, Seneca, Cayuga, and Oneida nations — formed a confederacy of five nations. They were united by the Law of Great Peace. The thirteen American colonies used this document as a model for the U.S. Constitution. Even the League's symbol of the white-headed eagle clutching arrows as symbols of nations and a pine bough as a symbol of peace were borrowed by the colonists. The only changes in the symbol were that the five arrows became thirteen and the pine bough became an olive branch, because Benjamin Franklin wanted to represent peace with a symbol that came from Europe. History books rarely teach these facts.

CHAPTER 9

←————→

An Answer

Are the American Indians immigrants to North and South America? The People say, "No. We watch scientists change the dates of when they think our ancestors arrived. Many now say 40,000 years ago. Some scientists say 100,000 years ago. A few scientists now believe we have, indeed, always been here. Years from now, maybe science will make up its mind."

For centuries Native American people have been called "savages." Their accomplishments have been destroyed when possible, otherwise ignored. Their cultures have been shredded. Their religious beliefs have been called myths. Their mother, the earth, has been abused.

Now they are called "immigrants." But they believe their hearts and what their ancestors have told them for thousands of years:

"We have always been here. We were created from the earth and her waters, and we progressed as a people on this land. We were influenced in our thinking and ways of life by the animals and birds from here. We were nurtured by the native plants, sheltered by the native trees, and inspired to live in peace by the spirits who dwell in these mountains. And the sky above us now, whether covered by dark, heavy clouds, or bright, blue air, has always been our Father. The twinkling and shining stars that we see at night, and those who travel from them and into our dreams, have provided stories, hope, and wonder for countless generations. They bear witness."

"All this, all this," the People say, "make us the true Natives of this land."

PART II

←——————→

Poets, Prophets, and Peacemakers Before Columbus

▼▼▼

CHAPTER 1

The Sacred Ones

▲▲▲

I, Nezahualcoyotl, ask this:
Is it true one really lives on the earth?
Not forever on the earth,
only a little while here.
Though it be jade it falls apart,
though it be gold it wears away,
though it be quetzal plumage it is
 torn asunder.
Not forever on the earth,
only a little while here . . . .

> —from the poet-king Nezahualcoyotl
> (1402–1472), the wise and famous
> lord of Tezcoco

Christians know how Christ, the son of God, wants them to live. Moslems know the sacred teachings that Allah gave to the prophet Mohammed. Buddhists have learned the ways of wisdom taught by Buddha. Christ, Mohammed, and Buddha are sacred beings, prophets among their people. They are holy and have supernatural qualities and powers.

Their teachings were recorded and have been practiced by their followers. The New Testament of the Bible is the story and teachings of Christ, the Koran describes the beliefs of Islam as they were told by Allah to Mohammed, and the Buddhist scriptures are documented in the language of India in the collection called the Canon, or "the school of the Elders," and in several languages of the Orient by Brahman priests.

These sacred beings sprang from the lands that gave their people birth. From these lands their religions were born. From the deserts of northern Africa and the Middle East and from the ancient mountains of Tibet, these religions were born. They did not come from America.

Here on this continent of North America, and in Central and South America too, there were sacred ones who walked the land and lived among the People. They too were teachers of wisdom, seeking unity, peace, and strength for their people. They were believed to be descendants of the sun and stars. Some of them were born of virgin women, making them supernatural also.

Native Americans recorded the existence of these great ones and their teachings in the poetry and prose of the written and oral traditions. The famous books of the Mayan priest Chilam Balam include the life of the cultural hero Quetzalcoatl. *Cuauhtitlan,* a manuscript written in Nahuatl, the ancient Aztec language, is one of a precious few books left of the great Indian libraries. Shortly after the Spanish arrived in the sixteenth century, the books were burned. The order for their destruction came from friar Diego de Landa. It was carried out by the Spanish conquistadors and the Catholic priests. Often, the Indian priests were hanged and made to watch while their libraries burned.

But, fortunately, something of the Toltec and Mayan and Aztec greatness survived through the written and oral traditions. Here in North America where there were no books, people became the books. The Iroquois Indians, like so many other tribes, passed down magnificent stories from generation to generation through memorization and the art of story-telling. To help them remember, they created colorfully beaded belts of wampum, a shell found in lakes and oceans. Like the surviving books of the Mayas and Aztecs, these are part of the library of Native America.

The poets wrote the books and the storytellers told the stories of the sacred ones who sprang from this land. Their beliefs and teachings flourished here.

Each sacred being was different. Each one lived at a different time and spoke a different language. The tribes or nations among whom each lived briefly were separated by thousands of miles, sometimes by whole continents. Each is also called by a different name:

Deganawida by the Iroquois, Quetzalcoatl by the Aztecs, Kukulcan by the Mayas, Manco Capac and Viracocha by the Incas, and White Buffalo Woman by the Lakota.

These heroes were real. They did live here, but there are few legends of their deaths. These sacred ones seemed to have disappeared after they succeeded in accomplishing their purposes.

According to one story, Deganawida, also called the Peacemaker out of respect for the sacredness of his name, left the People of the Longhouse in a canoe on the shores of a great lake. In another story, he went into an unknown region of the forest and wrapped himself in the bark of a decaying tree.

Quetzalcoatl, in some stories, floated away into the Gulf of Mexico on a raft of serpents. But in a Mayan book, the *Popol Vuh*, he ascended as fire into the sky. The next morning he reappeared as the morning star. To this day, Venus, the morning star, is believed to be the home of Quetzalcoatl.

According to Lakota belief, White Buffalo Woman changed into a white buffalo before rolling on the dusty earth and vanishing.

What happened to these sacred beings is often vague. But their accomplishments can be found all over the Western Hemisphere. Deganawida created a peace among the Iroquois Nations that still exists today. White Buffalo Woman's gift of the sacred pipe is seen every time an Indian raises a pipe of the sacred red stone to the heavens and prays to the Great Mystery for the protection of Mother Earth and for the well-being of the People.

These sacred beings also inspired magnificent art and grand architecture. Quetzalcoatl inspired the Toltecs, Aztecs, and Mayas to build great temples, even great cities. Quetzalcoatl's influence was so strong that he is said to be the inspiration for the incredible serpent mound in Ohio.

Citizens of North, Central, and South America should recognize the sacred places here where these sacred beings lived and taught. In this land holy places exist equally as sacred and splendid as any in the world. Some sacred sites are protected. Others have been ruined from lumbering, mining, or development. Still others were destroyed by some European Christians who saw these places as satanic.

Ancient stories of ancient places, ancient times, and ancient beings with supernatural powers are all part of the history of America. Upon this land walked poets, prophets, and peacemakers who influenced and changed the course of human history.

But what happened to the People after these sacred ones departed? How did the People manage to keep alive the ways taught to them by the sacred beings? One way they managed was through special men. These men kept the sacred teachings alive. They too are recorded in American Indian literature. Because they were mortal men who were not born with supernatural powers, they had to gain knowledge to help the People. They did this through fasting and concentrating on the Great Mystery for visions and dreams to help their people.

They were men of good heart, but they were only men. They had to rely only on their dreams and visions given to them by supernatural sources. They were simple men who lived humble lives uncomplicated by luxury and wealth. They were men of the highest order. Among them were Hyonwatha, the Delaware Prophet, Elkswatawa, Wovoka, Black Elk, and Lame Deer.

All of them, from Deganawida to Quetzalcoatl, from Hyonwatha to Lame Deer, were influenced by the Native American concept of the Giver of Life and by the land here in America. They were inspired by our mountains, our deserts, and our forests. They drew understanding from the stars scattered across the Sky which we call our Father and from the land we walk upon which we call our Mother. The animal nations that evolved here in America — the white-headed eagle, the grizzly bear, the white-tail deer, and the jaguar — spoke to these sacred ones and to the special men in their visions and dreams.

The Native cultures in the Americas are rich in knowledge. We all benefit from them in some way, but too often we know so little about them. The American Indian has proven that civilizations can be built in these lands where people can live happily and where clean cities and structures can be designed that are in harmony with the land.

Native Americans have proven that lasting peace can be established between nations and peoples. Such peaceful unions are rooted in the teachings of Native American peacemakers and cultural heroes. From these lands we can learn how pride and humility were woven into the artistic, political, and social achievements of the People.

These sacred ones and the special men, who helped the People live in harmony with each other and with the land, walked upon these continents. Some planted the seeds of light and understanding in the People's hearts and minds. Others nurtured those seeds and helped them to grow. They enabled the People to rediscover their center when it was lost to human flaw (weakness).

As they walked, they drank from these same waters that we drink from today, but the waters flowed clean and pure then. They also ate many of the same foods we now eat, all grown on this sacred soil. They meditated under the same stars we see in the night sky.

Some of the stories of these peacemakers and cultural heroes are still alive. So too are their beliefs: to live in peace and to prosper, be strong, and love the earth!

CHAPTER 2

Deganawida and Hyonwatha

▲▲▲

I, Deganawida, and the confederate lords now uproot the tallest pine tree and into the cavity thereby made we caste all weapons of war. Into the depth of the earth, down into the deep underearth currents of water flowing into unknown regions; we caste all weapons of war. We bury them from sight forever and plant again the Tree.

> —from a version of the Iroquois Constitution, as recorded in *Parker on the Iroquois*

▼▼▼

On December 25, in the United States, Canada, and in Central and South America, most people celebrate Christmas in honor of the birth of Jesus Christ. He has been called a prince of peace. He spoke of love, peace, and brotherhood. Unfortunately, today, in the land where he lived, the descendants of the People he preached among are dying from soldiers' guns and bombs.

Few people know that here in North America walked another prince of peace. He was called Deganawida. Together, he and the great orator Hyonwatha worked to establish peace among the Five Nations of the Haudenosaunee, or "People of the Longhouse." Today they are called the Iroquois Confederacy, or League of the Six Nations. They are the Mohawk, Seneca, Cayuga, Onondaga, Oneida, and Tuscarora. The Tuscarora joined years after the original league had formed.

Through his political genius, Deganawida devised a great peace for the Iroquois. Hyonwatha put it into words with his magnificent speaking powers. It is now the oldest living peace among nations in the world. It is recorded in the Law of Great Peace.

As a result of the Great Peace, the influence of the League of the Iroquois spread from the Northeast into Canada and as far west as the Ohio Valley. As a matter of fact, it is said that *Ohio* is an Iroquois word meaning "beautiful waters." That word, no doubt, referred to the lakes and rivers of Ohio when the Indians ruled the land. Many of those lakes and rivers are now polluted. In 1970, the Cuyahoga River that flows through the state of Ohio was so polluted, it was considered flammable!

The Law of Great Peace and the League of the Iroquois were created several hundred years before the arrival of any other race in this land. The Great Peace has survived the tests of the People. It has outlasted the European's arrival on these shores and his wars that were fueled by his religion and his idea of a "Manifest Destiny." The Law of Great Peace has endured as Deganawida had instructed, though its greatest test may be yet to come.

As a political document, the Law of Great Peace has served as a model and influence for the most powerful forms of government in the world today, including both democracy and communism.

Benjamin Franklin and Thomas Jefferson are just two of the United States' founding fathers who suggested that the colonies follow the kind of representative government the Iroquois had. The colonists' ambition was to break away from Mother England and to form a democracy with the thirteen colonies. Franklin made a special appeal for the Iroquois Confederacy's influence at the meeting of the thirteen colonies' representatives in Albany in 1754.

Marxism, which inspired the basic ideas of communism, was also influenced by Deganawida and Hyonwatha's Law of Great Peace. Karl Marx wrote about the Confederacy but died before including it in his famous *Das Kapital.* But Friedrich Engels, his successor and author of *Origin of the Family, Private Property, and the State* in 1884, wrote that the Law of Great Peace was "a wonderful constitution."

Engels went on to state that there were no needy or poor among the Indians. Everyone knew his or her responsibility to the welfare of all. All the People were equal and free — "the women included!" These were revolutionary ideas for Europeans.

Even Benjamin Franklin said that there was a special order of decency among the Indians, whom he referred to as "the savages." He marveled that these "savages" had no prisons and used no order, force, or any obvious means of punishment.

Are the peoples of the United States and the Soviet Union and China aware of the strong American Indian influence of the peacemaker Deganawida, expressed through the words of the orator Hyonwatha, on these two systems of government? Are the people aware of how profoundly The Law of Great Peace influenced the U.S. Constitution or of how the Indian tribal values influenced the ideals of communism?

The story of how Deganawida and Hyonwatha established the Law of Great Peace is told in the only living and truly North American epic. An epic is a long narrative (story) handed down by word of mouth from generation to generation. The *Iliad* and the *Odyssey* are examples of Greek epics. The *Satyricon* is a Roman epic, and *Beowulf* is an Anglo-Saxon, or English, epic. Even parts of the Bible were passed down orally before being put into writing. These treasures of literature began before there was a written language.

The *Epic of Deganawida* begins with Deganawida's birth from a virgin mother in a Huron village. He was born in a time when the People had lost their center. They were fighting so much that they began to believe the sun rose to give them power to fight. Nations fought nations, clans rivaled other clans. Even families fought families. Sometimes members of the same family fought each other. People were afraid to leave their longhouses at night for fear of being killed. Such was the time to which Deganawida was born. Such was the time when the People of the Longhouse had lost their center.

The epic story tells how Deganawida's mother named him. In a dream she was instructed to call him Deganawida. Only he was ever to have that name. To this day, the People of the Longhouse often call him "Peacemaker" instead of Deganawida, out of respect for his name. The People were instructed to use his name only when discussing the concepts of peace and his teachings.

His life among the People was filled with dangerous and trying adventures. Like his virgin birth, they revealed his supernatural powers. People know that fighting and killing are bad, but they will not let just anyone lead them away from such things.

His grandmother believed that the birth of a baby to a virgin woman must be some evil doing. People thought such things back then. Three times she stole away the child from his mother and threw him into a hole cut in the icy water. But each time the grandmother returned to the village, she found Deganawida suckling his mother's breast. Obviously, Deganawida had supernatural power. He could not be killed by drowning.

As Deganawida grew into manhood, he was noted for his pleasant appearance and handsome face. And he always spoke the truth. But back then, before there was a Law of Great Peace, the People had no place in their hearts for such a man who spoke of peace and love among men. The People sustained themselves by fighting. So, the People forced Deganawida away from the Huron village and the people of his birth.

When he was discovered by the Mohawks, or Flint Nation People, he was given a test to see if he really did have the power to establish the Great Peace. First, the Mohawks allowed him to select the means of his death. He chose to climb a tree and to suspend himself from a bough overlooking a great waterfall. Then, the Mohawks cut the limb, and Deganawida plunged into the swirling waters far below.

When he did not emerge, everyone who watched returned home. The next morning they discovered Deganawida smoking his pipe and cooking his morning meal. Indeed! He was the Peacemaker.

Deganawida stayed in the country of the Flint Nation, where he met Hyonwatha. Although Hyonwatha was a Mohawk, he had married an Onondaga woman. They had seven daughters. An evil sorcerer named Osinoh wanted Hyonwatha to leave Onondaga, so he killed the seven daughters. Hyonwatha was grief-stricken. When no one consoled him for the agonizing loss of his daughters, he felt even worse. Such is the way when people lose their center.

Hyonwatha then wandered far from Onondaga. He fasted in order to find his spiritual power. Finally, Deganawida relieved Hyonwatha's personal suffering. Now Hyonwatha was capable of assisting him in establishing the Law of Great Peace for the People.

The Mohawks were the first of the Iroquois nations to accept Deganwida's plan for peace. They considered it for some time before sending messengers to the other nations. One by one each nation joined the peace, for each nation realized that for its own protection and welfare it was the best thing to do.

Once the sovereign league of Indian nations had agreed on the peace, an eagle perched atop the tallest pine. This pine tree is forever called the Tree of Peace. The eagle can see far and observe any threats against the people of the Confederacy. If a threat occurs, the eagle at once warns the People. In his talons he clutches five arrows, symbols of the original Five Nations, and a pine bough, symbol of the Tree of Peace.

This symbol, like Deganawida's ideas of democracy and union, was borrowed by the founding fathers and is now a symbol of the United States. The only difference is the number of arrows in the eagle's talons, for the thirteen original colonies, and an olive branch, a symbol of peace from Europe and the Middle East.

The *Epic of Deganawida* is a marvelous literary account of the forming of peace in America. It has been largely ignored by teachers of American history and literature. American Indians have been insulted by teachers ignoring such important contributions. Probably a

greater insult came from the famous American poet, Henry Wadsworth Longfellow.

Longfellow composed a very popular poem, "The Song of Hiawatha." Unfortunately for us all, he had no consideration for historic truths. He changed the name Hyonwatha to "Hiawatha." Then he made Hiawatha an Ojibwa from the upper Midwest.

Longfellow was also incorrect in his geography. The Iroquois are from an area on the east coast of the United States now called New York. They also live just south of Montreal in the country now called Canada. Hyonwatha, no doubt, never set foot in Ojibwa country, which is in the land now called Minnesota, but that's where Longfellow placed him. Today in Minneapolis, Minnesota, there stands a huge statue of Hiawatha carrying his fictitious bride, Minnehaha, across a creek. Minnehaha is a Dakota Sioux word that means "Laughing Waters."

If this weren't enough, Longfellow almost called the poem "The Song of Manabozho" instead of "The Song of Hiawatha". Manabozho is the name of the supernatural Ojibwa trickster-hero. Longfellow decided on "Hiawatha" because he liked the name better. His also thought they both were the same person, anyway. How wrong he was!

Why is this important to know? One reason is that many students have to read "The Song of Hiawatha" in class. Another reason is to understand how the sacred ones and the special men of the American Indians are either unknown or incorrectly portrayed. Generations of schoolchildren have had to study and memorize one poem, and yet the real Hyonwatha and his accomplishments with Deganawida were omitted from American history and American literature classes.

Hyonwatha and Deganawida were native to this land. Together they accomplished great things. Unfortunately, most Americans remain ignorant of this special man Hyonwatha and this sacred being Deganawida.

CHAPTER 3

←——————→

Quetzalcoatl, the Plumed Serpent

▲▲▲

The Toltecs, the people of Quetzalcoatl,
were very skillful.

Nothing was difficult for them to do.
They cut precious stone,
wrought gold,
and made many works of art
and marvelous ornaments of feathers.
Truly they were skillful.

All the arts of the Toltecs,
their knowledge, everything came
from Quetzalcoatl . . . .

And those Toltecs were very rich,
they were happy;
there was no poverty or sadness.
Nothing was lacking in their houses,
there was no hunger among them . . . .

> —from *Cuauhtitlan*, an ancient manuscript recorded in Nahuatl, the Aztec language

▼▼▼

Who was he that is said to have descended from the sky as a plumed serpent only to take the form of a bearded fair-skinned man hundreds and hundreds of years ago? Who was this cultural hero that others said was born of a virgin woman and who swallowed a stone of jade? His name is Quetzalcoatl.

He influenced every Native American culture of ancient Mexico. Just north of present-day Mexico City in the state of Hidalgo, in the Valley of Mexico, is the ancient city of Tulan (now called Tula). Possibly the most beautiful city ever created, this is where Quetzalcoatl lived.

Toltec art and literature during the time of Quetzalcoatl has never been surpassed. Even the name Toltec has come to mean "great works of art."

These Toltecs, considered the most artistic and poetic of peoples, called themselves the People of Quetzalcoatl. Even today, a person who strives to create beauty with art or literature is called a Toltec among many of the Indians of Mexico, regardless of nationality.

The Toltec golden age ended when Quetzalcoatl, the lordly prince of Tulan, was forced to flee from conspiring wizards. He headed east (some stories say) to the land of the Mixtecs. There one can see evidence of his influence in the sculptures and paintings in the temples. Under his influence, the Mixtecs built the largest pyramid ever found in the world.

In Teotihuacán, also located in the Valley of Mexico and about twenty miles northeast of modern Mexico City, ruins have been uncovered that the Toltecs said were created by giants. It was here, more than 1,500 years ago, that the mysterious Toltecs made their original home. It was America's first great metropolis. The city was magnificent with its wonderfully decorated stone and wooden buildings, great colorful temples, and large ball courts where games were played. It even had wide thoroughfares connecting the parts of the city.

This was Teotihuacán! It was the place of the most awesome structure ever built, the Temple of the Sun. And at the end of a thoroughfare called the Avenue of the Dead stands the striking Temple of Quetzalcoatl, embraced by sculptures of winged and feathered serpents.

According to the Aztecs, who later rebuilt Teotihuacán, the fifth and present age of the world emerged there. It is called the Age of Quetzalcoatl.

So who was he that many anthropologists and historians often refer to as a myth? Could a myth have such influence? The People know who he was. His presence is recorded in their blood and made visible in their literature and art. He was known as Quetzalcoatl by most, as Kukulcan by the Quinche Maya, and as Viracocha by the descendants of the Inca. He was the plumed serpent. He became a man. He was a cultural hero!

The ancient stories say he brought corn to the People and instructed them in finer methods of farming. They say the People never wanted for anything while he was their prince and lord. He revitalized their arts. He discouraged human sacrifice to their gods, because he preferred butterflies and flowers instead. It is said that this is why the wizards eventually drove him away from his beloved Tulan. The wizards believed that human sacrifice should continue if the the sun was to allow life.

Sacrifice was a way of returning the blessings of light and warmth and life — all that the sun provides — in order to ensure the survival of the People. Because the body is all the Indian ever felt he owned, this was his greatest gift. It made for strong nations.

The Plains Indian nations of North America practiced the sacred Sun Dance. In this ritual, men suspended themselves from the trunk of a cottonwood tree on ropes tied to bones pierced in their breasts. Thus they danced before the summer sun until their flesh was torn, releasing them and returning their spirit energy to the sun for the goodness of their people.

The People knew that life is a kind of energy. The People were aware of their responsibility to live in harmony and balance with nature. They believed that the sun and the earth, which always provide for us in this life, must have something returned to them or their power would cease. The People and the world as we know it would be no more.

So, the ancient Indians of Mexico and Central America offered humans in sacrifice. It wasn't done all the time. Such sacrifices were not even done every year. But in times of need, they were performed. And this is what Quetzalcoatl discouraged. He knew the Indians' understanding of life cycles and power, so he persuaded them to give back other things.

Quetzalcoatl taught that creativity is a way of giving back to the gods some of the life energy provided for the People. The Giver of Life created the gods, he explained. Then the gods created the sun and the rain to sustain life in this world. Thus, Quetzalcoatl deemed that man should learn from their example and create beauty also.

As horrible as human sacrifice sounds today, it was better than the Europeans' methods of war at that time — burning, raping, and slaughtering men, women, and children. The European armies cut off the heads and other parts of their enemies and placed them in exhibition. The disarmed Aztecs at Tenochtitlán were butchered at the hands of the Spanish in the name of "Christianity."

At some point Quetzalcoatl left his people. One version is recorded in a Mayan book, the *Popol Vuh*. He entered a great pyre of flames while birds of all nations and colors came to witness. They and the People watched as the smoke rose to the heavens. At dawn the next day the People observed the appearance of the morning star. There they believe Quetzalcoatl now lives. He is that world.

The other version of Quetzalcoatl's departure from the world describes him traveling east on the Gulf of Mexico in a raft of colorful serpents. This version tells of his predicted return. That date coincided so closely with the arrival of the Spaniards that the frustrated and bereaved Aztec king Moctezuma II allowed the Spaniards entrance to his city, thus beginning the slaughter and demise of the Aztec nation.

According to the Aztecs who wrote in Nahuatl under the watchful eye of friar Bernadino de Sahagun, there were ten omens foretelling the conquest of Mexico. Miguel Leon Portilla recorded these omens in his book *Broken Spears*. The omens occurred ten years before the arrival of the Spanish. One omen told of a weeping woman who could be heard late at night crying loudly: "My children, we must flee away from this city. My children, where shall I take you?"

Many stories have been told and retold through the centuries. Some ring as true as an Aztec poet's words. Some are stories of valiant Native heroes; others are of the invaders. Some tell of the clash between two worlds and of the two ways of seeing the same world.

When the Catholic missionaries, particularly Diego de Landa, observed the great sculptures and temples erected in the name of the Plumed Serpent Quetzalcoatl, they immediately assumed that the People were devil worshipers. The missionaries had the Aztecs and Mayas killed or Christianized, destroyed the cities, and burned the libraries! In an abuse of the name of Christ, a prince of peace, one of the world's greatest cultures disappeared.

CHAPTER 4

From the Sun — the Great Mystery

He was descended from the sun and was born to the place that still bears the name Island of the Sun. The island is located in Peru on Lake Titicaca, the highest lake in the world. He was the first Inca, and his name was Manco Capac.

Citizens of the United States and citizens of Canada recently and proudly celebrated 200 and 100 years of government, respectively. The Golden Age of the Incas, however, lasted at least 300 years, and the Incas completed a broken tradition of government that had lasted for thousands of years.

Although some historians write of imperial wars of the Incas, what cannot be denied is that they also spread their influence without violent acts of aggression. Like the Iroquois under the influence of Deganawida, the Incas spread their empire mainly by attraction.

Manco Capac instructed all the kings who were to follow him that at no time must they spread his influence and their nation by the blood of others. They were to attract the Indians with benefits of all kinds. He said the Inca should conquer with love. The Inca Nation of Manco Capac was absent of war. They had no slaves.

Like other Indian nations, including the Aztecs, the Incas addressed the awesome power of the sun, but they did not worship the sun. They regarded the sun as the living descendant of Pachacamac, meaning "the Giver of Life to the Universe" or "the Great (Holy) Mystery." The sun was addressed with songs and prayers and sometimes sacrifice.

The Incas neither worshiped gold and silver nor considered them to be a sign of wealth. Gold to the Inca was a symbol of the sun like the cross is a symbol of Christianity and the Star of David a symbol of Judaism. Gold to the Inca was the "sweat of the sun." It was worn as an outward sign of human humility before this mighty power of light and warmth.

Although the Incas were great architects of stone and sculptors of precious metals, they are most noted for their agricultural accomplishments. The Incas alone have contributed more to the world by means of food and medicine than all the countries of Europe combined. After the "New World" was discovered by the Europeans, Native American foods nearly wiped out the famines that had plagued Europe for centuries and allowed for a population explosion in Europe. According to many scientists, Incan food staples, which were probably cultivated for the first time at the Incan city of Machu Picchu, make up over half of the world's food staples today. These staples include potatoes, corn, beans, and tomatoes.

These accomplishments came about due to the wise Inca descendants of Manco Capac and the teachings and gifts of Viracocha. It is believed that Viracocha was the same sacred being as Quetzalcoatl of the Toltecs and Aztecs and as Kukulcan of the Quinche Mayas. He is described as a fair-skinned man who was seen from time to time walking on the mountain roads with a staff (walking stick). He was a cultural hero who brought many gifts and much knowledge to the People!

Like the Toltecs, Aztecs, Mixtecs, and Mayas, the Incas built a temple in his honor. It is the Temple of Viracocha, and it rests near the Pacific coast in Ecuador.

CHAPTER 5

White Buffalo Woman

With this holy pipe you will walk like a living prayer . . . your feet resting upon your grandmother, the pipe stem reaching all the way up to the sky to the grandfather, your body linking the Sacred Beneath with the Sacred Above.

— from Lame Deer's retelling of White Buffalo Woman's words to the People

▼▼▼

The pipe that White Buffalo Woman brought to the Ikce Wicasa (the human beings) is ages old. It is still kept by these Lakota (Sioux) Indians and is the most sacred of all their sacred things.

Lame Deer, a Sioux medicine man, describes it in the book *Lame Deer, Seeker of Visions*, which he wrote with

Richard Erdoes. The ancient pipe is wrapped in red flannel and buffalo wool. Tied to it are "red eagle feathers, four small scalps, and bird skins." Made from the leg bone of a buffalo calf, it is not like any other pipe.

With this pipe, White Buffalo Woman showed the Indian how to pray. It might well be the first pipe ever used.

Ages and ages ago, during a particularly fine summer day when the grasses were green and high on the plains, the People were hungry. There was not enough meat. So, two hunters were chosen to go out and search for the buffalo.

When they saw something move on the hill, they became anxious. It seemed to be a buffalo. As they approached it, though, the form that moved on the hill turned into a beautiful young woman. Her dress was of white buckskin and decorated in a way that no human could have done. Her hair hung long and loose, except for a part of it that was tied with buffalo hair. On her back was a bundle. In her arms she carried a fan made from the leaves of wild sage. She was the most beautiful woman either hunter had ever seen.

She told them not to be afraid, for she was from the buffalo nation. She told them she had something good for the People.

It is said that while she spoke, one of the hunters became obsessed with desire and wanted her. When he reached to touch this most beautiful woman, who was more than human, a mist fell over him. When the mist-cloud lifted, dried human bones lay where the hunter once stood.

As Lame Deer explains, there is more to this encounter, but one thing is certain: "Desire killed that man." And, as we can see from our knowledge of the past, desire and lust, whether it be for another's life or country or gold and money, has killed many people.

The other hunter returned to the People and described what happened. They prepared for White Buffalo Woman, and she came. She came and taught them the use of the living pipe by using it to pray to the Great Mystery.

She spoke to the women and explained their relationship to the welfare of the tribe. She spoke to the men, warriors and hunters alike, and explained how the sacred pipe binds all men and women in a circle of love. It binds all things together as relatives to one another.

She spoke to the children and explained how they were wiser than their years because they were still so close to the Great Mystery. She told them that they were to be respected as equals and that what their parents and other adults did was for them, the children. She told them that they were the future. They were to remember these things so they could teach their children for all generations to come. Only in this way would the People continue.

When she was done speaking, she took the bundle from her back and unwrapped the sacred pipe. She gave it to an elder man to protect and keep, for no one can own a pipe, one can be only a protector and keeper.

As the People watched her leave, she turned into a white buffalo and disappeared into the horizon.

ABOUT THE AUTHOR

Noted author and lecturer Gabriel Horn was given the name "White Deer of Autumn" by his uncles, Metacomet and Nippawanock, and by Princess Red Wing of the Narragansett tribe, Wampanoag nation. He has taught in reservation schools, American Indian Movement (AIM) survival schools, public schools, and junior colleges. He helped develop the curriculum and was head teacher at the Red School House in St. Paul, Minnesota. He was cultural arts director of the Minneapolis American Indian Center from 1980 to 1982 and helped establish the Minneapolis American Indian Art Gallery and the Living Traditions Museum. For his work in Indian rights, he was nominated for the Human Rights Award in the state of Minnesota.

Gabriel Horn has a master's degree in English and currently devotes his time to lecturing, teaching, and writing. He is a teacher in Florida as well as a member of the National Committee on American Indian History and an advisor to the Native American national newspaper, *Indigenous Thought.* He lives on the Florida coast with his wife, Simone, an Ojibway, close to Mother Earth and the natural world that is so precious to him.

ABOUT THE ILLUSTRATOR

Shonto Begay is a Native American artist who specializes in multicultural illustrations. His other works include *The Mud Pony,* a Native American story, and *Lluvia,* a Hispanic children's book. He lives in Kayenta, Arizona, with his family. His illustrations for *Native People, Native Ways* accurately detail the traditional dress, architecture, and art of the many different Native tribes in the various regions of the Americas throughout history.

ACKNOWLEDGMENTS

The "Native People, Native Ways" series would not have been accomplished without the support and assistance of my wife, Simone, and the sacrifices made by my loving children: Ihasha, Calusa, and Carises. Without Jay Johnson's belief in my work and Paige Graham's ability to work with draft after draft of each manuscript, and without Paige's constant reminders for me to listen to the ghost voices, these books would not reflect the quality that they have. I'm also grateful to the publishers of Beyond Words, Cynthia Black and Richard Cohn, who recognized the quality of the series and the needs that the books can help fulfill. Their proofreader, Marvin Moore, and Native American curriculum specialist, Chris Landon, fine-tuned the books in such a way as to make us all proud. And to Fred Brady and the other elders who sent their prayers into the Mystery that these books would become a reality for our children and grandchildren, I give my deepest gratitude. I would also like to thank my friend and agent, Sandra Martin, who continues to encourage me to write. I'm grateful to Shonto Begay for his spark of creativity that will help children to see Native people in a Native way. And lastly, I wish to acknowledge all the elders who took the time to teach me, and all the writers whose spirit enabled them to share what they too have learned from the Native People and Native Ways of this land.